DATE DUE

DEMCO 38-296

People to Know

John Grisham

Best-Selling Author

Kathy Ishizuka

Enslow Publishers, Inc.

40 Industrial Road	PO Box 38
Box 398	Aldershot
Berkeley Heights, NJ 07922	Hants GU12 6BP
USA	UK

http://www.enslow.com

Library of Congress Cataloging-in-Publication Data

Ishizuka, Kathy.
  John Grisham : best-selling author / Kathy Ishizuka.
      p. cm. — (People to know)
  Summary: Discusses the life, career, and influence of the popular writer of legal
thrillers.
  Includes bibliographical references and index.
  ISBN 0-7660-2102-5
  1. Grisham, John—Juvenile literature. 2. Legal stories, American—History and
criticism—Juvenile literature. 3. Novelists, American—20th century—Biography—
Juvenile literature. [1. Grisham, John. 2. Authors, American.] I. Title. II. Series.
  PS3557.R5355Z74   2003
  813'.54—dc21

                                                    2003000700

Printed in the United States of America

10 9 8 7 6 5 4 3 2 1

Illustration Credits: AP Worldwide Photos, pp. 40, 79; Center for Steinbeck
Studies, San Jose State University, p. 14; Classmates Online Inc., p. 12;
Corbis, pp. 23, 24; Delta State University, p. 16; Department of
Defense/Defense Visual Information, p. 20; Dover Publications, Inc., p. 13;
Tom Drysdale, p. 92, John Grisham Papers, Special Collections
Department, Mitchell Memorial Library, Mississippi State University, p. 30;
Library of Congress pp. 7, 57, 78; Little League Baseball, Inc., 97;
Mississippi Development Authority, p. 10, 30; Mississippi State University,
pp. 19, 82, 88, 96; Square Books, p. 60; That Store in Blytheville, pp. 46,
51, 64, 72.

Cover Illustration: Deborah Feingold

Contents

Southern Loyalty Tour

John Grisham was sitting on an airplane, en route to a promotional appearance for one of his popular thrillers. A flight attendant approached his seat in first class and said, "There's a request from the back of the plane for you to sign a book."

"Sure," replied Grisham, who willingly gave his autograph.

Word spread through the plane, causing a flurry of activity in the aisles, as passenger after passenger made the same request. "That's enough," said Grisham. "Get all the books together and we'll have a book signing." Grisham does not remember how many books he signed that day. But "It was a lot," he said. "It was a big jet."[1]

Other novelists have surely enjoyed seeing a fellow passenger reading one of their works. But only John Grisham could suddenly decide to hold a book signing on a commercial flight and have fans lining the aisles.

John Grisham's novels are so popular that humorist Dave Barry once declared that a Grisham paperback could double as a boarding pass. With more than 100 million copies in print in thirty-one languages, Grisham is quite likely the best-selling novelist of all time.

He is a master of the legal thriller, and his fast-paced novels have arrived like clockwork early each year since 1991. So far, seven Grisham novels have been turned into feature films—*The Firm, The Pelican Brief, The Client, A Time to Kill, The Rainmaker, The Chamber,* and *The Runaway Jury*—furthering his extraordinary commercial success.

But this former country lawyer has never forgotten his roots. With the release of each of his books, Grisham has returned to five Southern bookstores, which offered him encouragement and support when he was just starting out as a writer.

"It is totally unusual for an author of his stature to do signings," said Marion Seith, a representative from Doubleday, his publisher.[2] Grisham is so popular that he could easily stay at home and still sell millions of copies. Yet he sits for hours at each store, signing books for some of his most loyal fans.

People come from as far away as Chicago and even England to attend a Grisham signing. High school teachers bring students by the busload. Although

Grisham never fails to have a book signing in his hometown of Oxford, Mississippi. This Civil War monument stands in the middle of town.

they may wait as long as ten hours for a book-signing ticket, many are repeat customers who make the annual trek to meet their favorite author. Many consider Grisham an old acquaintance.

Grisham's appearances on his "Southern loyalty tour" are largely good-natured, orderly affairs. But tickets run out quickly, and fans must be turned away. Some beg, while others even cry. For the disappointed ones, Grisham always stays to sign a few hundred extra copies of his books. And on one occasion at Burke's Book Store in Memphis, he stepped outside to meet a fan who was left standing in the pouring rain.

Grisham makes few public appearances. But he is always pleased to visit these local bookstores. It is his way of recognizing the booksellers, the fans, and the entire region that helped make him the popular author that he is. As people are known to say of Grisham, he has not forgotten where he came from.

John Grisham's popularity as a writer is unparalleled. As amazing as any tale he could have imagined, the extraordinary rise of this small-town southern lawyer is one of publishing's most fascinating success stories.

Dreams of Glory

John Ray Grisham, Jr., was born in Jonesboro, Arkansas, on February 8, 1955, the second child of Wanda and John Grisham, Sr. As a youngster growing up in the farmland of northeastern Arkansas, John would pick cotton when schools closed for the harvest. It was hard, hot work. While young John never dreamed of becoming a writer, of one thing he was certain. He would never be a farmer.

When John was about seven years old, his father gave up the struggling cotton business and joined a traveling construction crew. The family moved frequently across the South, settling briefly wherever John senior could find work. Crenshaw, Mississippi; Delhi, Louisiana; and Parkin, Arkansas, are some of

While living in Arkansas farm country as a small boy, Grisham would pick cotton during his school breaks. This cotton gin is one typically used by farmers.

the towns Grisham called home for a brief time. Although they moved around often, "it was a lot of fun," said Grisham.[1]

The family did not have much money. But John and his four siblings were never left wanting. "We were well fed, and loved and scrubbed," he said.[2] They enjoyed all the simple pleasures of childhood, particularly on the baseball field, where John developed a lifelong love of the game. At home John would glue himself to the radio, listening to baseball and dreaming of playing for his favorite team, the St. Louis Cardinals.

With their frequent moves, the Grisham children were accustomed to change. There was always a new church, a new school, and new friends. So they learned to adapt quickly. Upon their arrival in a new town, the first order of business was to join the local Baptist church. Next came a visit to the library, where the Grishams would get their library cards and check out as many books as they could. John, of course, also checked out the local Little League field.

The Grisham children could size up a town by the library's check-out limit. Some towns let you take out two or three books, and others, four or five. "And one town was eight, which we thought was pretty awesome," said Grisham.[3]

With their father often working seven days a week, it was Wanda Grisham who provided John and his siblings with constant care and guidance. She discouraged television; there was reading and story-telling instead. On his father's side was "a family of storytellers," said Grisham. There were "long dinners and lots of stories. As children, we absorbed them."[4] Their mother also insisted on church every Sunday.

One day, when he was eight years old, John said to his mother, "I need to talk to you." "We talked, and she led me to Jesus," said Grisham. "The following Sunday I made a public confirmation of my faith. In one sense, it was not terribly eventful for an eight-year-old. But it was the most important event in my life."[5] John's religious faith would sustain him from that day forward.

In 1967, when John was twelve, the Grishams moved to Southaven, Mississippi. A quiet suburb of Memphis, Tennessee, Southaven would become the family's permanent home.

While in school, Grisham's greatest interest was in athletics. He dreamed of being a professional athlete. Grisham graduated from high school in 1973.

Mark Twain was one of Grisham's favorite authors.

Although John was passionate about baseball, he was not as enthusiastic about school. He was indifferent about his studies and did not care at all for writing. "I never dreamed of becoming a writer when I was a kid," said Grisham. "I never thought about it. So my only training was having read a great deal as a child and always having loved books."[6] Among John's early favorites were Dr. Seuss, the Hardy Boys, *Emil and the Detectives*, Chip Hilton, and the novels of Mark Twain and Charles Dickens.

In his teens, John discovered the work of John Steinbeck through his high school teacher, Francis McGuffey. The first book that really grabbed him was a book that Miss McGuffey assigned called *Tortilla Flat* by Steinbeck.[7] John particularly liked Steinbeck's realistic style of writing and shared his enthusiasm with his teacher. McGuffey then "fed" John other Steinbeck books, from *Of Mice and Men* to *The Grapes of Wrath*.

The powerful *Grapes of Wrath* had a tremendous impact on John. Set in the 1930s, Steinbeck's novel centers on the Joads, a family of farmworkers who fight poverty and hardship as they migrate from the

John Steinbeck, whose work made a strong impression on Grisham, receives the 1962 Nobel Prize in literature.

drought-stricken "Dust Bowl" of Oklahoma to California. "I don't know if it had anything to do with my writing style, or me as a writer, because I wasn't thinking about it back then. It had a lot to do with the way I viewed humanity and the struggles of little people against big people. It was a very important book for me."[8]

Steinbeck, who won the 1962 Nobel Prize for literature, remained a lifelong favorite of John's and would influence Grisham's own writing in the years to come.

Despite his enthusiasm for reading, John earned a D in English composition. His grades in other subjects were also unimpressive. Still, his teachers at Southaven High School took note of John's self-confidence and drive—if only he would apply these qualities to schoolwork. Instead he focused mainly on sports and pursuing girls.

John was set on becoming a professional athlete, although at the time, he had not decided between baseball and football. He had not distinguished himself in either sport, yet he was certain that he was destined for glory. Much to his surprise, no college appeared interested in drafting him into its athletic program. His career in sports should have ended there, but he did not give up.

John graduated from high school in 1973. He had hoped for an athletic scholarship to a major college or university. But when none came, John had few options. So he decided to enter Northwest Mississippi Junior College in nearby Senatobia. (Grisham later admitted that he was unprepared for college.)

He spent a year mostly playing baseball, in the position of right field. But, in truth, he spent most of the time on the bench. After that, he felt confident enough to move on. In the fall of 1974, he transferred to Delta State University in Cleveland, Mississippi, to play for Coach Dave "Boo" Ferriss.

Ferriss, a local baseball legend, began his impressive career at Mississippi State University in the 1940s, then went on to pitch for the Boston Red Sox. In 1946, he led that team to the American League pennant and won the coveted Cy Young Award. After a coaching stint at Boston, Ferriss arrived at Delta State in 1960, where he had head-coached winning teams ever since.

With dreams of professional glory, John took his place on the team. But one day, as he stepped up to the plate, something happened that would change those dreams forever. "I watched in horror as a fast ball came directly at my head at 90 M.P.H.," said Grisham. "It missed, but I was sick at my stomach. The next pitch was a bit slower but nonetheless headed straight for my ear. I immediately dived toward third base and did not see the ball as it dropped and

Legendary coach Boo Ferriss helped convince Grisham that he did not have a future in professional baseball.

curved beautifully across the plate. I faked back spasms and crawled to the dugout."[9]

John was humiliated. The very next day, Coach Ferriss called him into his office. As gently as he could, Ferriss informed John that he was not up to playing college-level baseball. Specifically he could not hit a fast ball, nor a curve. So, John was dropped from the team.

Although Ferriss had tried to steer John toward his studies, John did not heed his advice, at least not immediately. John had paid almost no attention to academics, and his grades showed it. Very soon he and his roommates, who had become close friends, grew restless. They talked about trying forestry together or going to Appalachia College to experience the mountains. At the end of that semester, the merry gang left Delta State to sample yet another local college.

In 1975, John wandered onto the campus of Mississippi State University in Starkville. He was a young man with no real plans and seemingly very few prospects for the future. Despite his experience at Delta State, John still fantasized about a career in the major leagues.

A patient woman in the admissions office sorted through John's sparse college record and admitted him to Mississippi State. Little did John realize that this marked a significant occasion for him. For in the coming years, he would find direction in his life and finally grow up.

Grisham
Gets Serious

When he arrived at Mississippi State University, John Grisham, the student, did not make much of an impression. The few grades that he was able to transfer from Northwest and Delta State were poor. He had moved around so much that even his parents had trouble keeping track of which college he was attending.[1] But Grisham himself did not seem to care. After all, he was just passing through.

Grisham settled on finance as his major and arrived at his first class: economics. Little did he know, as he took his seat, that he was about to witness something that would wake his mind and forever change his attitude toward his education.

During the class, the professor expressed his political views on Vietnam, the controversial war in

Grisham transferred to Mississippi State University in 1975 with no real plans. This is the MSU library as it looks today.

Southeast Asia in which the United States joined South Vietnam in fighting the communist-ruled North. This sparked a heated response from his students. Grisham looked on in amazement as his well-spoken classmates, including two Vietnam veterans, fearlessly confronted the professor.

"Of course, I contributed nothing to the discussion. I hadn't even purchased the textbook," said Grisham. "But at that moment, in my first class at State, I became a student—not a radical, but a kid who suddenly wanted to grow up and learn."[2]

He bought the textbook, but after just two weeks, Grisham dropped the class. Economics was simply not for him. Still, Grisham continued to work hard at improving his grades. He even began to consider the possibility of entering law school. His roommates could not believe their eyes as they watched their friend transform into a serious student. He worked hard, taking notes and writing papers. He made a habit of attending class and started reading *The Wall Street Journal*, *Forbes*, and *Fortune*.

Taking a break from his studies, Grisham made his first attempt at writing fiction. He started a piece based on a journal in which he had jotted down several story ideas. This first effort, Grisham admitted,

Grisham was inspired by fellow MSU students who were knowledgeable about the Vietnam War. Here, U.S. Marines land in South Vietnam in March 1965.

was not very successful. It was so bad that he would only reveal that the plot concerned a small town in Mississippi. When spring arrived—baseball season—Grisham would sit in the stands of Dudy Noble, MSU's baseball field. Watching the players made him a little sad. He dearly missed the game. But one day, as he looked out onto the field, Grisham finally decided "it was time to grow up, to stop dreaming of the World Series and adoring masses, to get a degree and then another, to simply get to work. When I left the bleachers that night, I was no longer a boy."[3]

By the time his roommates decided to leave school, Grisham was faced with a decision. Would he continue their "merry adventure" of sampling schools? Although he was sorry to see them go, he decided to remain at Mississippi State. Grisham said good-bye to his buddies, who would remain lifelong friends.

In 1977, Grisham received a B.S. degree in accounting from Mississippi State. The next year, he entered the University of Mississippi Law School. With his sights set on a profitable career, he decided to become a tax lawyer. In contrast to his earlier days as a directionless student, Grisham now had a plan: He would make a fortune representing rich clients. But then he encountered his first course in tax law. The complex subject completely turned Grisham off. Once again, it was a field that did not suit him.

He then turned to criminal defense law. As part of their training, law students would participate in a mock courtroom, where Grisham discovered he had a natural talent. "[I was] very, very good on my feet," he observed.[4] In one "case," Grisham was called on to play a drunk who was on trial for murder. Grisham got into the part—as Slimey Caldwell, he showed up in a scraggly beard, wearing a T-shirt that said "Drink Till You Puke." The student lawyer who defended Slimey had to work very hard, indeed, because Grisham was so convincing in the role.

Grisham could not get enough of the experience and would sneak out of class to watch actual trials. People in court, he observed, reveal things that they would not otherwise air in public. The drama of the courtroom would forever fascinate John Grisham.

While in law school, Grisham took another stab at creative writing. He started the first chapter of a novel, which involved a terrorist plot at an American college campus. Grisham planned to complete the novel before he graduated from law school. But it took a month for him to produce the first chapter. Without getting very far, he dropped the project.

Around this time, Grisham was pleased to hear from a close pal from his Mississippi State days. But then his friend delivered some shocking news: He was ill with terminal cancer. Grisham was in disbelief. "What are you going to do?" he asked his friend, who eventually died at age twenty-five. He said, "It's real simple. You get things right with God, and you spend as much time with those you love as you can. Then you settle up with everybody else."[5] This encounter deeply affected Grisham and would influence the priorities he made in his own life.

A newly mature John Grisham had a significant year in 1981. He graduated from the University of Mississippi Law School with a J.D. (Juris Doctor)

At Mississippi State University, Grisham decided to pursue a career in law, so that he could work in courtrooms such as this one.

degree and was admitted to the Mississippi bar. It was also a special time in his personal life.

"For years she was a little girl next door," said Grisham of Renee Jones, who had also grown up in Southaven. She was "too young to notice. When I came home from college, she was the prettiest woman you ever saw in your life."[6] Grisham, then twenty-six, had found a life partner in twenty-year-old Renee. The two married on May 8, 1981—the week after he graduated from law school—in Oxford, Mississippi.

The couple settled in Southaven, their hometown.

For years Renee Jones was just the "girl next door" for Grisham.
They married in 1981. They are shown here at a state dinner.

There, in a small downtown office, Grisham opened a one-man law practice. He specialized in criminal law, representing people charged with armed robbery, assault, and drug possession, among other crimes.

In his first murder case, Grisham was appointed by the court to defend a man who shot his wife's boyfriend six times at close range. Just nine months out of law school, the inexperienced Grisham was a nervous wreck in court. The trial went so badly that even his own client slid as far down the defense table from Grisham as he could get. Then it came time for the closing argument.

A shaky Grisham stood and requested permission to approach the bench. The judge leaned forward and whispered, "Do you need to go vomit?"[7] With that, Grisham ran out of the courtroom. When he returned, he managed to collect himself and then turned to address the jury.

First, Grisham apologized for his performance and asked the jurors not to hold it against his client. He then proceeded to make a case for self-defense, based on the fact that the dead man had fired a small-caliber weapon at his client. Grisham grew more confident as he went along. By the time he sat down, the judge gave him an approving wink.

Then came the announcement that the jury had reached a decision. Grisham rose to his feet as the foreman read the verdict—"Not guilty." His client had been acquitted. Grisham was elated.

Soon, however, the young lawyer found it difficult to make much of a living representing average people; that first case paid just one thousand dollars. So

Grisham switched to more lucrative civil, or private cases.

A highlight of his career occurred when he represented a boy who was burned over 90 percent of his body when a water heater exploded. Grisham won the case, one of the largest damage settlements ever recorded in De Soto County. He proudly displayed the water heater in a glass case in his office.

From his earliest days as a lawyer, Grisham found it especially gratifying when the "little guy" beat the odds and won against the "big guy," whether it was a big corporation, law firm, or other powerful entity. It was a theme as old as David and Goliath, but one that inspired Grisham and his future work as a writer.

John Grisham built a successful law practice, often putting in up to eighty hours a week at his office. His hard work earned a comfortable life complete with a nice three-bedroom home and a pool. But Grisham wanted more.

In 1983, Grisham decided to enter politics. Dedicated to improving education in his state, Grisham ran as a Democrat and was elected to represent Mississippi's Seventh District in the state legislature. He continued to practice law while he worked three months of the year in the House of Representatives. His schedule was so grueling, Grisham would later refer to the 1980s as a blur.[8]

Grisham was known as a serious politician interested in making change for the better. But politics proved frustrating. He soon realized that despite all his good efforts, the tedious workings of government made it almost impossible to accomplish anything.

There were rewarding moments in both politics and law, but much of the time, Grisham was just plain bored. On Fridays, he began to play hooky with fellow attorney William Ballard. The two would meet in Oxford, where they enjoyed discussing literature over coffee at Square Books.

Yet again, Grisham found himself at another crossroads in life. According to Renee, John still didn't know what he wanted to be when he grew up.[9]

In the meantime, the Grishams became a family. In 1983, Renee and John celebrated the birth of their first child, a son named Ty. John was delighted to be a father. But while things were going well at home, Grisham was growing increasingly discouraged with his work.

In his first year as an attorney, Grisham had found the practice of law rewarding. He had achieved his college goal of making a good living. Now he yearned for something more fulfilling. But he didn't yet know what that was.

As he climbed the steps of the DeSoto County courthouse one day, Grisham could not expect that what he was about to see would change the course of his life. But as he walked by a courtroom, he happened upon a trial that captured his attention like no other.

First-Time Author

On that fateful day, John Grisham saw a young girl on the witness stand, testifying against the man who had brutally raped her. It was a gut-wrenching experience for Grisham, who stayed and watched. "One moment she was courageous, the next pitifully frail. I was mesmerized," he said.[1] Grisham was overtaken with so many emotions—sympathy, hatred, pity, revenge. If that had been his daughter—he could only imagine a father's rage. What if the girl's father killed the rapist and was put on trial for murder?

With that dramatic situation as a starting point, Grisham's imagination took off. A story began to build in his mind. It became his obsession for three months, in which he thought of little else. How would a jury treat such a father? Grisham wondered. Would they be sympathetic enough to acquit him of murder? It was a situation ripe with suspense and drama. He added his own twists and turns in developing the story, based in part on his own experiences as a criminal lawyer.

Late one night in 1984, Grisham began to put it all down on paper. He wrote the story in longhand, scribbling on a legal pad, the type used by court reporters. The first page came quickly, then the second, and before he knew it, he had completed the first chapter of a book.

Grisham showed the first chapter to Renee, who would become his most important critic. "Renee reads five or six novels a week," said Grisham, "and she has little patience with a story that doesn't work."[2] Although he felt confident about the story, Grisham was not as sure about his writing skills. He was encouraged when Renee asked to read more. After the next two chapters, Renee was hooked.

From then on, there was no stopping Grisham. He completed at least a page a day, under all conditions. "I wrote with the flu, on vacation, with no sleep, in courthouses when I could sneak off to a quiet room for 30 minutes, in the state capitol building in Jackson," he said.[3] He admits having his doubts, but he never gave up on the book. It was always on his mind.

Grisham rose at 5:00 in the morning to write at home. "People would drive by and see me working and think I was this workaholic lawyer, which was great for business," he said.[4] By 9:00 A.M. he was back in

In 1988, Grisham was elected to his second term in the Mississippi House of Representatives. Grisham is seated (below, center) with other legislators of the Northeast Mississippi coalition in 1990.

his law office. Grisham kept his project very private—no one knew about it except his wife.

At first, Grisham looked on writing as just a hobby. "Because I have the problem of starting projects and not completing them, my goal for this book was simply to finish it," he said. Getting published was the furthest thing from his mind. "Then I started thinking that it would be nice to have a novel sitting on my desk, something I could point to and say, 'Yeah, I wrote that.'"[5] With Renee's encouragement, he kept on going.

A year passed, when Grisham realized he had collected an impressive pile of manuscript pages—enough for half a book. "I caught myself thinking of publishing contracts and royalty statements and fancy lunches with agents and editors—the dreams of every unpublished novelist," he said.[6] Grisham had been bitten by the publishing bug.

Despite his busy schedule and budding career as a writer, Grisham always gave priority to home and family, which grew again in 1986 when Renee gave birth to their second child, a daughter named Shea.

In 1987, three years—and more than twenty handwritten pads—after he had started the project—John Grisham finished his manuscript. He had accomplished his goal of seeing a project through. Even more remarkable than that, he had written his first novel. But he did not stop there. Next came an even bigger challenge—getting it published.

When he first realized he had a potential book on his hands, Grisham knew that he needed to learn more about the publishing process. So as he worked on his manuscript, he read everything he could find on the book publishing industry.

In January 1987, as he prepared to go to Jackson for the opening session of the Mississippi legislature, Grisham swung into action. What had started out as a hobby was about to become an all-out campaign.

With the help of his secretary, Grisham set about creating two lists. One had the names and addresses of thirty editors, the other, thirty literary agents. After typing the handwritten manuscript, his secretary would send a summary of his book and the first three chapters to the first five editors and the first five agents. When a rejection came back, the name would be crossed off the list and a new package immediately sent to the next name. With this system, Grisham made sure that his work kept circulating.

What he did not plan on was receiving so many rejections. A total of twenty-eight publishers and agents declined his story. This might have discouraged many people, but Grisham says that it never got him down. "I never thought of quitting," he said. "Honestly, I believe I would've sent it to several hundred people before I would have even thought of giving up."[7] A few months later, Grisham's determination would pay off.

In April 1987, John Grisham got the phone call he had been hoping for (from agent number sixteen). Jay Garon, a literary agent from New York, introduced himself and said that he wanted to represent Grisham and his manuscript. This meant that Garon would show the manuscript to publishers, with the goal of making it into a book. Garon wanted to mail a contract right away, and Grisham accepted. It was a memorable moment for the author. As for Garon, he was sold immediately on the project—originally titled *Deathknell*—saying it revealed "a great sense of tempo" and "had the authenticity of someone who had been there."[8]

The new author was so eager to sell his book that he called his agent frequently. Garon's first piece of advice to his client: Stop calling and start writing another book. Grisham took the direction and set to work on a story right away.

All this time, Grisham was still working his "day job," practicing law. In 1988, he was reelected to a second term in the Mississippi House of Representatives. He had become the vice-chairman of the Apportionment and Elections Committee and held memberships on several other important committees, including military affairs.

Although Grisham worked hard at representing his district and on important issues, such as education reform, he realized that there was a lot of wasted time in government. In these spare moments, he would take out a legal pad—which he always kept handy—and find a quiet place to write. Soon, these pads filled up with Grisham's creative work.

For a year, Garon made the rounds with Grisham's project. No one, it seemed, wanted to take a chance on a new writer.

Then in 1988, Garon received a call from editor Bill Thompson of Wynwood Press. He wanted to publish Grisham's book. Thompson was building a reputation for discovering authors. Years earlier, he had bought another first novel, *Carrie*, by then-unknown writer Stephen King.

For the rights to publish his book, the publisher paid Grisham a $15,000 advance. While this was merely a fraction of the money he would receive later in his career, his first publishing contract remains a highlight for Grisham. "When you get that first phone call from New York and someone says your book is going to be published, the feeling is incredible," he said. "I've had a lot of big calls since then, but none felt bigger."

After signing his first contract, Grisham got to work with Wynwood editors, who suggested changes in his manuscript. For the novice author, it was a new experience to be edited. But Grisham believes the editors helped strengthen the book's characters and improved his work. He revised the manuscript many times before it was finished. Grisham also came up with a new title—after six or seven tries.

A Time to Kill was published in June 1989. Opening with the brutal rape of a ten-year-old black girl, the book centers on the trial of her grieving father, after he murders the two white rapists on the courthouse steps of Clanton, a fictional southern town. A young attorney, Jake Brigance, defends the father before an all-white jury, sparking racial hatred and violence. As he tries to save his client's life, Brigance himself is threatened by the Ku Klux Klan, the secret organization dedicated to white supremacy.

It is said that first novels tend to be autobiographical. That is the case with *A Time to Kill*. The author admits that he and Brigance share a lot in common.

They are both street lawyers. In *A Time to Kill,* Grisham describes these lawyers, who, unlike big-money corporate attorneys, "picked up the scraps and represented people—living, breathing human souls, most of whom had very little money. These were the "street lawyers"—those in the trenches helping people in trouble. Jake was proud to be a street lawyer."[9]

"Jake and I are the same age," adds Grisham. "Much of what he says and does is what I think I would say and do under the circumstances. We've both felt the unbearable pressure of murder trials . . . We've both lost sleep over clients and vomited in courthouse restrooms."[10]

The publisher printed a modest five thousand copies of *A Time to Kill.* Grisham bought one thousand himself. After giving some away to family and friends, he carried copies in the trunk of his car and sold them at local garden-club meetings and libraries.

The book was not very well promoted by the publisher, so Grisham tried to publicize the book on his own. He approached local bookstores around Memphis and the mid-South about giving him a book party. Only a handful agreed to help the unknown author and his equally unknown book. They included Richard Howorth of Square Books in Oxford, Mississippi.

Grisham told Howorth that he needed to sell five hundred copies. But the bookseller cautioned Grisham not to expect too much. "Look," he said. "If we invite your mama and your wife, your friends and all your relatives, we will do well to sell 50 copies."[11]

Howorth was not far off the mark; Square Books sold fifty-three copies at the book signing.

At another reception, Grisham was set up with a stack of books at a table in front of the bookstore. Hardly anyone showed up. "People walking by would veer away from me like I was a beggar," said Grisham. "A buddy of mine from law school finally walked by and we talked for an hour and a half. And he didn't even buy a book."[12]

Although the first edition of *A Time to Kill* was not a best-seller, Grisham would never forget the local bookstores and their support of him.

But the book earned respectable attention from critics. They praised Grisham's ability to tell a lively story and his treatment of the racial theme. "The characters are salty and down-to-earth," wrote David Keymer in *Library Journal*. "An enjoyable book, which displays a respect for Mississippi ways and for the contrary people who live there."[13]

"This one came from the heart," said Grisham of *A Time to Kill*. "It's better [than my other books] because you can almost smell the biscuits and the eggs and the grits and hear the chatter in the Coffee Shop; the people are better . . . you can feel the sweat sticking to their shirts in the July heat around the courthouse."[14]

It was a notable achievement, but Grisham's first publishing experience was just the start of things to come.

The Big Break

With his second book, Grisham decided to go in a completely different direction. *A Time to Kill* was a regional story, he thought, which also could be a reason it did not sell well. This time he wanted to entertain readers, and, frankly, sell some books. So he decided to try his hand at a fast-paced thriller. In *Writer's Digest* magazine, Grisham discovered an article with the rules of suspense, which he committed to memory. With these rules as his only instruction—Grisham had never taken a course in writing—he began to outline a story.

Then, as he had with his first idea, he approached Renee. This was always a little frightening, as Renee is so tough, she "makes those people in New York [book editors] look like *children*," says Grisham.[1] He knew he had just enough time to blurt out the story idea, before Renee delivered her opinion. "She loves to shoot them down, which really irritates me," Grisham said.[2]

But when he described his story about a young lawyer who joins a Memphis firm connected to the mob, Renee said, "Wait a minute. That could be a big book."[3] After that, Grisham spent six months on an outline and then began writing *The Firm.*

As was now his habit, Grisham got up at 5:00 A.M. to start writing. He had to carve out this time, since he was still putting in sixty to seventy hours a week at the office and spending three to four months a year in the legislature.

Grisham admits that he was not as motivated during the writing of his second book. And the poor sales of *A Time to Kill* contributed to his self-doubt. He would enter a bookstore and see all those books and think to himself, "Who would be interested in reading my story?" He had also heard that Americans were not reading as much as in the past. "There are always thousands of reasons not to do something," he said. "You can always think of more reasons not to do it than to do it."[4]

Grisham says that he would play little games with himself to get the work done. He would tell himself he had to be at his desk by 5:30. And in the first thirty minutes, he had to have his first page written. At midday he would take an hour break to have lunch with Renee. The two discussed John's progress every day. By the time a book comes out, Renee has read it at least five times.

Grisham kept up this disciplined schedule. Two years and countless revisions later, he completed the manuscript for *The Firm* in September 1989.

The Firm tells the story of Mitchell McDeere, a young law school grad, who is enticed into joining the Memphis firm of Bendini, Lambert & Lock. With the offer of a huge salary and a new BMW car, Mitch believes he has it made. But the job is too good to be true. After some of the firm's lawyers die mysteriously, Mitch learns that it is an operation run by an organized crime network. All the lawyers are involved in concealing the illegal profits of the mob, a scheme otherwise known as money laundering. The Mafia will kill McDeere if he leaves the firm, and if he refuses to act as an inside informant for the FBI, they will put him in jail.

Grisham's own experience in law school inspired the plot of *The Firm*. While he was an average student, Grisham had friends who were academic stars. Like Mitch, they were pursued by law firms at graduation.

Grisham recalls how these classmates would get together and compare the packages offered to them by big firms in Memphis and New Orleans. He would enjoy listening to them say, "We don't know these lawyers. What if they're up to something?"

Grisham's imagination took off from there, leading to a plot rich with intrigue. A friend from college who was an investigator for the Internal Revenue Service helped him with the details of illegal financial dealings. Grisham set the book in nearby Memphis, partly for lack of time and money to study another location. But he also admitted being a lazy researcher.

Tom Cruise starred in the movie The Firm, *based on a book by Grisham.*

Grisham sent the finished manuscript to his agent, and Garon decided to hold an auction. Garon then contacted several editors, offering them the chance to bid on the publishing rights. They politely declined the opportunity. Like Grisham's first book, *The Firm* initially met with a round of rejections.

Then, the author got the biggest break of his career. "I didn't even know about it," he says.[5]

It was like something out of, well, a thriller novel. A movie scout had somehow secured a copy of *The Firm*, and Grisham's manuscript was being circulated in Hollywood, without the author's knowledge.

On a Sunday morning in January 1990, the Grishams were on their way to church. Renee was running late, when the phone rang. John had gone on ahead to buy juice for his preschool Sunday school class. When he arrived at church, an excited Renee told him to call his agent right away. It was Garon asking John for his permission to take the highest offer from Disney, Paramount, or Universal for the film rights to *The Firm*.

Stunned, Grisham gave the go-ahead and returned to church. After sitting through what seemed like an endless sermon, followed by three baby dedications, he arrived home, when Garon called back. Paramount had bought the film rights for $600,000. "I asked my agent how he got that kind of money for it," Grisham told a reporter, "and he just said, 'I'm a helluva agent.'"[6]

Overnight, Grisham had become a hot property. The previously neglected manuscript for *The Firm* now had eighteen publishers begging for the chance to publish it. "It was a hoot," said Grisham.[7]

Within two weeks, publishing rights were sold for $200,000 to David Gernert, an editor at Doubleday, which had previously declined *The Firm.* Grisham still has the rejection letter. Doubleday also had Grisham sign a contract for three more books.

The combined deals for *The Firm* changed John Grisham's life. He and Renee now had the financial means to build their dream house. And he could become a full-time writer.

From there, "it was fairly easy to close the office down and run all the clients away," said Grisham.[8] After working as a full-time lawyer for almost ten years, Grisham had no regrets about leaving his practice. "When I started law school, I thought I could do some good when I got out, help people who needed help and make a decent living at it," he said. But he had become discouraged with the profession. And his practice no longer stimulated him.

He gave the office furniture to his child's kindergarten, but kept the computer—a basic model Smith Corona word processor—and copy machine. These items were moved into a more permanent area for writing, which he set up in the laundry room of his home.

Grisham then resigned from the Mississippi legislature, saying he had never intended to serve more than eight years. He made the announcement in September 1990, halfway through his second term. "In the past several years, I have found it nearly impossible to devote a reasonable amount of time to my legislative duties, and at the same time, be a husband, father, lawyer, and now, a writer," said Grisham, then thirty-five years old. "Something had to give."[9] Although he would never again serve in office, Grisham maintained an active interest in politics and important social issues.

But quitting his "day job" was a risk for Grisham. *The Firm* would not be published until spring 1991, and its success was not at all assured. Nevertheless, he was eager to take the plunge into full-time writing. "For me, writing has gotten to be a habit," said Grisham. "And I think I'd like to do it all the time."[10]

On that Sunday in January 1990, John Grisham became a wealthy man. And the book that made it happen would not be published for a year. Nothing like this had ever happened before in the publishing world. As for Grisham, the experience was completely unreal.

John and Renee Grisham considered their options and decided they could live anywhere they wanted. He imagined a private office where he could write. No longer would Grisham have to work in a narrow space crammed between the washer and the dryer, where he would be forced to take a break when it was time to move a load of laundry from one machine to the other.

So the couple picked up the family and moved to Oxford—not far from Southaven—where Renee could finish earning her English degree at the University of Mississippi. They bought a seventy-acre property, a former thoroughbred horse farm, complete with barns and two ponds stocked with fish. There, Renee's father, a contractor, began building their dream house on the crest of a hill. The two-story yellow Victorian mansion included the private office that Grisham had coveted.

Grisham also enjoyed being part of the Oxford community. The picturesque town was famous as the home of Nobel Prize–winning novelist William Faulkner, who lived there from 1918 until his death in 1962. Oxford has been home to countless authors ever since.

From his new home base, Grisham concentrated on family. Life for him and Renee centered largely on the kids. There were school activities, baseball, of course, and a menagerie of animals, including cats, rabbits, ducks, snakes, and a retriever named Bo. On Sundays they attended Oxford's First Baptist Church, where they were married. Despite his sudden wealth, life really had not changed very much.

Like a Whirlwind

In March 1991, Doubleday released *The Firm*. In contrast to Grisham's first book, *The Firm* was launched with a first printing of 55,000 copies and a publicity campaign. There were advertisements and author appearances, and advance copies were sent to bookstores. In a unique ploy, the publisher also targeted the legal community, sending excerpts of *The Firm* to law journals.

In a separate deal, Grisham signed a contract with film production company Enchanter Entertainment for *The Gingerbread Man*. This original screenplay, Grisham's first, concerned a southern attorney's entanglement with a female client.

Meanwhile, *The Firm* was earning favorable reviews, although some critics noted that Grisham's characters lacked depth. Critic Pagan Kennedy said that in *The Firm*, Grisham "concentrates less on his characters than on their conspicuous consumption—BMWs, silk ties, BMWs, solid-cherry desks, BMWs . . ."[1] Aspects of the plot were unbelievable, said Peter Prescott of *Newsweek*, "And yet the story has significant strengths. It also offers an irresistible plot."[2] What impressed critic Bill Brashler was Grisham's ability to show the schemes of the bad guys as well as the hero. "This is not a mystery, but a well-paced and, at times, harrowing thriller." *The Firm* reads "like a whirlwind," wrote Brashler.[3]

Apparently, readers also found *The Firm* hard to put down. It became a favorite among booksellers,

John Grisham is joined by his mother, Wanda, (third from left) and aunts at a book signing.

who spread the word among their customers that the book was a real page-turner. Just weeks after its publication, *The Firm* made it onto *The New York Times* best-seller list. It debuted at number six, and by the second week of April, the book had climbed to number three. Grisham later commented that while *The Firm* was not his first book, "it was the first book anybody read."[4]

It seemed that Grisham had achieved his goal of gripping readers with a fast-paced plot. "I was determined to write clearly," he told a *Washington Post* reporter. "When you write suspense, you want it lean, fast. There's a conscious effort to keep people up all night."

Lawyers, especially, were enthusiastic about *The Firm*. Grisham thinks they were pleased that he—a former lawyer—wrote it and was able to leave the profession. "It was as if I had gone over the wall and escaped and they wished they could, too," he said.[5]

After making the best-seller list, Grisham was compared to another successful former lawyer-turned-writer, Scott Turow. In 1987, Turow published his first novel *Presumed Innocent*, which he wrote during his daily commute to his job as a Chicago district attorney. A murder mystery involving a lawyer, *Presumed Innocent* was a huge hit and is credited with popularizing the legal thriller.

Grisham acknowledged Turow's book as a classic of its kind but denies any close comparison. Grisham says that he sent the first draft of *A Time to Kill* to his agent a month before *Presumed Innocent* was published. "There's plenty of room for both of us," he said.

"And in the end, the good books sell, and the bad ones don't."[6]

In the wake of his first big hit, Grisham was often asked why he thought people liked *The Firm*. He cited the book's suspense, which readers seemed to get caught up in. Grisham also believed that *The Firm* had a broader appeal than his first book.

In addition, *The Firm*'s lack of objectionable content allowed people to recommend the book to their older teens or parents. "I was really pressured by my editors to put in more violence and sex in *The Firm*," said Grisham. "It's a real struggle to capture some degree of realism in fiction and stick as close as possible to your convictions. Sex is a gimmick because it sells. To me it's a challenge to write and sell without it."[7]

The Firm remained on the best-seller list for an amazing forty-seven weeks. At first, Grisham said, "all I wanted was for it to stay on [the best-seller list] one more week—it would be embarrassing if it fell right off. But I never dreamed of all this."[8] Although it never held the number one spot, *The Firm* became the biggest selling novel of 1991. More than 600,000 copies were sold in hardcover, and the book was translated into twenty-nine languages.

Even after *The Firm* had become a huge success, Doubleday kept up its publicity campaign. Grisham agreed to a national book tour. But he disliked the spotlight.

But his extraordinary and sudden success had transformed Grisham into a public figure overnight. Here was a man who would have preferred to stay on his Mississippi farm and mow the grass, but he found himself traveling to New York City to be interviewed on the nationally televised *Today Show*.

Grisham approached his predicament with a degree of humor. The book was doing so well, he told Doubleday that he had better stay at home or he might screw up a good thing. And in April 1991, when he learned that he had the number-three best-seller, Grisham told a reporter that he was actually more excited to be named head coach of his seven-year-old son's Little League baseball team.[9]

Grisham, however, was serious about maintaining his privacy. Despite all the excitement surrounding *The Firm*, he retreated to his Oxford home.

Grisham also needed to get back to work. Doubleday was quite eager to follow up the huge best-seller with another book. This time, Grisham felt a certain pressure that he had not experienced during the writing of his earlier books. The media was also interested in learning more about his next project. When pressed about its title, Grisham told a reporter it is *The Third Novel*.[10]

With this book, Grisham turned his attention to the Supreme Court. He considered the last liberals of the high court, Justices William Brennan and Thurgood Marshall, and how a sitting president would seek to replace them. So began the premise for *The Pelican Brief*.

Although he normally shunned research, Grisham did his homework for this book. He studied maps of Washington, D.C., and walked through Dupont Circle and other settings he would use in his book. He cased the streets of Georgetown, where, in his new book, a Supreme Court justice is murdered in his home. To grasp the life of a reporter—a key character in his book—Grisham hung out in the newsroom of *The Washington Post*. He tried to get the floor plans for the Supreme Court and the FBI but aroused suspicion and was turned down.

The manuscript was due in August, so Grisham tacked this date up on the wall. This would become a tradition with all his books. Even his kids knew what this meant—do not bother dad. Grisham would then hole up in his office and write, producing an average of ten pages each day. At night, he edited and proofread his work.

In the summer of 1991—when Grisham was only halfway through the manuscript—filmmaker Alan Pakula purchased film rights to *The Pelican Brief*. Grisham continued writing and made his August deadline, producing a completed novel in just one hundred days.

A string of Grisham books hit the stores in 1992. The paperback edition of *The Firm* was released in January. Then in March came his new book, *The Pelican Brief*. Another legal thriller, *The Pelican Brief* tells the story of Darby Shaw, a Tulane University law student, who investigates the murder of two Supreme Court justices. The intelligent, long-legged Shaw proposes a conspiracy theory in a paper called the "Pelican Brief." After passing the brief to the FBI, Shaw's law professor-boyfriend is killed in a car bombing. Shaw is then sent running for her life,

The books keep moving as Grisham fans wait in line to meet the legal-thriller author.

threatened by the FBI in a conspiracy that extends all the way to the White House.

Almost immediately, *The Pelican Brief* skyrocketed to the top of the best-seller charts. Doubleday initially printed 425,000 copies, then three more printings followed in quick succession. Meanwhile, Grisham signed a contract with Doubleday to publish his next three books. The deal would earn the best-selling author $6 million. By the publication of *Pelican*, Grisham was already well into the manuscript for his next book.

In March, Grisham embarked on an eighteen-city book tour. He would cover two or three cities each week, doing interviews and making appearances across the country to promote *The Pelican Brief.* It was a hectic schedule, during which he flew home on weekends.

Although he disliked the national appearances, Grisham always made sure to stop by five local bookstores in the South that had supported him in his early days as a first-time author. Stops on his so-called "Southern loyalty tour" included Square Books in Oxford, Reeds Gumtree Bookstore in Tupelo, Mississippi, and That Bookstore in Blytheville, Arkansas, not far from his birthplace of Jonesboro.[11]

"I've gone back with every book," he says. "I call them my home stores. Now the book signings last for 10 or 12 hours, but you know, it's still fun."[12] Seeing the long lines of fans that extended outside the stores, it seemed impossible that just a few years ago barely a soul showed up for a Grisham signing.

John Grisham Knocks Out John Grisham

While sales soared, *The Pelican Brief* drew mixed views from critics. Several called the plot formulaic. "*The Pelican Brief . . .* is as close to its predecessor as you can get without running *The Firm* through the office copier," wrote John Skow of *Time.*[1] Others called the characters simplistic. Once again, Grisham was accused of paying too much attention to superficial details, namely Darby's appearance and how often she changed her hair color.

Grisham bristled at the criticism. Reviewers had been kind to him in the beginning. Now that he was a commercial success, he believed they were out to get him.

In Grisham's opinion, *The Pelican Brief* was as good as *The Firm* and perhaps even more suspenseful. As for

Renee, *The Pelican Brief* was her favorite of John's books. She was especially proud of John, who proved to her in this story that he could create a strong female character. "I'm not trying to write serious literature," said Grisham. "This is not 'art.' I'm trying my best to write high-quality, popular fiction. That's all . . ."[2]

Indeed, a Grisham book is first and foremost entertaining—on that fans and critics agree. To that end, Grisham follows three rules in his stories: Hook readers with a gripping start, maintain tension throughout the middle, and follow through with an ending so exciting that people will stay up all night to finish the book.

Grisham stories usually center on a bright, driven individual swept up in a dangerous conspiracy. The situation must threaten their lives—a necessary element in suspense. To keep readers pulling for them, Grisham makes the protagonist, or hero, a likeable, sympathetic character. Although Grisham admitted that Mitch of *The Firm* was perhaps a little too greedy.

Always, a Grisham hero is pitted against a powerful, evil enemy. This theme recalls Grisham's lawyer days, when he sided with the "little guy" against the rich and powerful. For Grisham—the former defense attorney—fiction is a chance to "get back at people, chew 'em up: big law firms and insurance companies, arrogant judges and lawyers."[3]

The legal profession is a never-ending source of inspiration for Grisham. "We [lawyers] see so much—a weird case, a crazy client," he said.[4] Although he had long since given up on it as a full-time career, Grisham remained passionate about the human drama of the law. He continued to stay in touch with the field, following cases and even accepting one or two clients each year.

Grisham was particularly fascinated by the real-life schemes of crooked lawyers. Some took their client's money and disappeared. Another even faked his own death and showed up at his own funeral. Certain true-life cases would have Grisham considering "What if?" and a story idea would build from there.

Many lawyers, inspired by the success of Grisham and Scott Turow, tried their own hand at creating a legal thriller. In 1992, Grisham's agent received 117 manuscripts written by attorneys. This was no surprise to Grisham, who believed that most lawyers would rather be doing something else. He imagined lawyers in courtrooms and law offices across the country, grabbing a spare moment to scribble their stories, as he once did. He encouraged their efforts at fiction, believing that every lawyer has a story to tell.

Meanwhile, excitement was brewing in Hollywood over *The Firm.* In April 1992, it was announced that Oscar-winning film director Sydney Pollack would direct. Gossip buzzed about who would play the plum lead role. In a May interview, actor Tom Cruise let it slip that he would portray Mitch McDeere. Grisham was pleased. There was no one better, he felt, to play his hero.

Grisham's success renewed interest in his first novel. *A Time to Kill,* the book closest to Grisham's heart, was re-released in July 1992, first in paperback, then in hardcover. That same month, *The Pelican*

Brief was the number-one fiction best-seller, while *A Time to Kill* and *The Firm* were the biggest-selling paperbacks.

"They're trading places with each other for number one," said Roger Bilheimer, publicity director for Dell, of the paperbacks. "John Grisham knocks out John Grisham who knocks out John Grisham."[5] For a single author to simultaneously occupy these top spots was a rare feat in publishing.

Around this time, a reporter visited an airport terminal and asked the first ten passengers he encountered what they were reading. Four were carrying *A Time to Kill* and one was halfway through *The Pelican Brief.*[6] Grisham, it seems, was also the top author at twenty-thousand feet.

John Grisham, at thirty-seven years old, was a certified superstar. By the time *Pelican* came out, publicity efforts centered as much on the author as the book. With his smooth southern manner and blue-eyed good looks, Grisham attracted many fans. Women, especially, found him appealing. His wholesome lifestyle and devotion to his family only added to his charm.

But Grisham remained a reluctant celebrity who shied away from all the attention. He was eager to finish touring to get back to his pet project: building a baseball field on his property. So far, he had finished home plate and the backstop. He was even more delighted to return that spring as coach to nine-year-old Ty's Little League team.

Grisham also enjoyed hanging out at Oxford's Square Books, where he had signed his first copies of

A Time to Kill. There he got to know Larry Brown, Barry Hannah, and other local writers.

His peers could have resented his wealth and fame. But Grisham was, by all accounts, a nice guy, well liked by his Oxford neighbors. They also respected his privacy. "Obviously I'm a different kind of writer," he said, referring to his unique status in the community as a millionaire best-selling author. "I take what I do seriously, but it's not serious."[7]

But living in Oxford, Grisham could not escape comparison with the novelist who put the town on the map, the late, great William Faulkner. Acknowledging Faulkner as an extraordinary literary artist, Grisham found the comparisons with himself, a writer of popular fiction, ridiculous and unfair.

Grisham expressed his frustration in a 1992 article he wrote for the *Oxford American* entitled "The Faulkner Thing." It is an amusing account of an aggressive television reporter who confronts Grisham at a book signing and tries to make a connection between him and the Nobel Prize–winning author. Grisham is clearly fed up.

"How do you compare yourself with William

William Faulkner was another author who lived in Oxford.

Faulkner?" wrote Grisham. "A handful of morons have asked me this question, and nothing irritates me more."

Yet "the Faulkner thing"—which inevitably raised questions about the quality of Grisham's writing—would continue to haunt Grisham. This made the shy celebrity even more wary of reporters.

Grisham completed the *Pelican Brief* tour in May 1992 and returned to his home and the fourth book project. Once again he resumed his strict work schedule, rising at dawn and writing for at least six hours each day. Even when he took a break to fish, go jogging, or ride his tractor, he would be thinking about the next scene in his book. Grisham completed the manuscript for *The Client* by September 1992. It had taken him just six months to write.

The Client centers on an eleven-year-old boy, Mark Sway, who tries to stop a lawyer's suicide, but he learns a terrible secret that endangers his life. In the book's riveting opening, the dying man tells the boy that his gangster client has murdered a U.S. senator. The lawyer's death leaves Mark the only person alive who knows the truth about the case (and where the body is buried). Enter Reggie Love, a street lawyer and grandmother, who steps in to protect the boy from both the mob and the FBI.

The Client's young hero is a tough survivor, who helped his mother escape his abusive father. While working on the book, Grisham called on his instincts as a parent. "Would an 11-year-old be that smart?" he asked himself. "I'd think of my son, who was then 9, add two years, and say 'Sure.'"[8] As Grisham polished a second draft, it became clear that the compelling drama of *The Client* was perfect for the big screen.

Jay Garon arranged an auction to sell film rights for the new story in October 1992. In a posh Los Angeles hotel, the agent set up a fax machine and five telephone lines to handle calls from bidders. Four major movie studios and several smaller ones all vied for the book. Grisham was frequently consulted during the lively negotiations, which extended over several days. Famed producer Dino De Laurentiis offered $1.5 million. Paramount and Warner Brothers submitted their own high bids. Finally, on October 11, 1992, producer Arnon Milchan's New Regency Productions won the auction for $2.5 million. It was believed to be the highest price ever paid for film rights to a novel.[9]

After the sale, Grisham settled down to polish the third draft of *The Client*. He had concentrated on developing the characters, partly in response to criticism of his earlier books. "When reviews are negative but fair, I pay attention," he said. "Some said my characters were shallow—and they were. *The Firm* and *The Pelican Brief* are very fast, plot-driven books."[10] He admitted sacrificing some of the suspense in order to flesh out better characters in *The Client*.

Grisham vowed to stay away from the film production. Although *The Client*'s big sale landed him on *Entertainment Weekly*'s list of the 101 most influential power people in entertainment, his response was "I'm going to stay on the farm."[11]

From the beginning, Grisham's instincts kept him from getting involved with the movies. He had never

For nine years in a row, these Grisham fans have been the first in line for Grisham signings at Square Books in Oxford, Mississippi.

been much of a fan, and was known to walk out of the theater during films he particularly disliked. He also seldom watched television.

Grisham was not happy with early scripts for *The Firm*, which differed greatly from his story. But once the book was published and became a best-seller, filmmakers decided to stick more closely to the original plot.

Grisham also wanted *The Firm* to maintain a PG-13 rating. But knowing he had little control, Grisham remained concerned about the content of film versions of his work, particularly graphic scenes of sex and violence. While the film deals fueled his popularity, John Grisham would continue to have an uneasy relationship with Hollywood.

Meanwhile, filming of *The Firm* was set to begin in Memphis that November. Things were crazy enough, thought Grisham, who was just learning to cope with a certain loss of privacy. He wondered, what was going to happen when the movies came out?

The Grisham Business

By February 1993, John Grisham's books had sold altogether 17 million copies. With the March publication of *The Client*, Grisham once again climbed to the top of the best-seller charts, where he also claimed the three top-selling paperbacks. Meanwhile—showing no signs of slowing his pace—the author was already hard at work on his fifth novel.

In just a couple of years John Grisham had become a major industry all by himself. He was ranked thirty-first among the world's richest entertainers, according to Forbes magazine, with an estimated 1992–1993 income of $25 million. Without giving away the actual figure, the author claimed that it was actually much more.

A Grisham blockbuster was now an annual spring event, eagerly awaited by his publisher and the entire book industry, which profited greatly from his success. Bookstores around the country cleared shelf space in anticipation—a new Grisham book easily sold one thousand copies a day. And film producers competed to get a first peek at his next manuscript.

Grisham was also credited with "singlehandedly making it really cool for lots and lots of people to read," said Mary Gay Shipley, owner of That Bookstore in Blytheville, Arkansas. People who had not opened a book since high school told Shipley how much they loved the latest Grisham. They then asked her to recommend other titles. "Sometimes I feel that Jesus could come back and sign the Gospels, and my customers would rather know about John Grisham's latest book," she said. [1]

Grisham's fans also included kids. "I love John Grisham," said fourteen-year-old Kristen Hoppe. "I call the bookstores to see when his next book is coming out. I count the days. *The Firm, The Pelican Brief.* I've read all of them." [2]

Grisham was highly aware of his own status. Although he did not like to talk about money—not a polite topic for a southern gentleman—Grisham had carefully tracked his standing on best-seller lists since *The Firm.* He also knew how much his publisher depended on him. As for all the little stores, such as Shipley's, their very existence relied on his producing an annual bestseller.

Grisham's current project, *The Chamber,* was the first in a four-book contract with Doubleday that

John Grisham always returns to his hometown bookstore for signings. He is pictured here with "That Bookstore" owner and manager Mary Gay Shipley.

committed him to producing a book a year. In March, film director Ron Howard and producer Brian Grazer paid a record $3.75 million for film rights to *The Chamber* on the basis of a one-page summary.

"The words and ideas are coming fast," said Grisham, "and for now a book a year is easy."[3] But such speedy production did not enhance the quality of Grisham's writing. Again, critics said he relied too heavily on a formula plot in *The Client.* Grisham admitted that he had rushed the writing of *The Pelican Brief* and *The Client*, which was completed in just six months.

Grisham had a reason for keeping up this pace. He believed that his success would not last forever. "It's going to be over one of these days, like the career of an athlete," he said. "When it is, I hope I can say it was fun, and that I kept both feet on the ground."[4]

Grisham was, in fact, remarkably unchanged by his sudden fame and wealth. The constants in his life remained the same, including his devotion to his family and the Baptist church.

Grisham's faith had been an important part of his life since childhood, and he remained actively involved in the local congregation. He attended services with his family each Sunday. It was the only occasion that he shaved, so as not to offend the ladies in church, who might not approve of a days-old beard. John and Renee regularly taught Sunday school and also participated in missionary work.

In April 1993, Grisham joined a group of forty church members on a mission to Brazil. It was something he had wanted to do for years, but never had the chance to because of his busy law practice. In a remote part of the country, the group planned to build a small chapel and supply health care and medicine to a needy community.

Upon arriving in Brazil, Grisham was shocked by what he saw. He witnessed the extremes of human existence, from incredible wealth in Rio and other big cities to unbelievable poverty in the villages. The author was moved by the experience. Grisham returned to Brazil several times.

In May 1993, Grisham was back home when filming began on *The Pelican Brief.* He had assisted director Alan Pakula in selecting the New Orleans locations.

Set to play the lead character, Darby, was Julia Roberts, the premiere actress in Hollywood. Roberts had liked the book so much that she wrote a fan letter to Grisham and expressed her interest in appearing in the movie. He believed Roberts was perfect for the role.

The next month, *The Firm* premiered at a star-studded New York event. It was a very emotional moment for John and Renee, as they sat down to watch the opening credits of the first Grisham film adaptation. It was, after all, the book that had made his career. And Renee, his most trusted advisor, had been with him at every step leading up to this moment.

Featuring Tom Cruise, Gene Hackman, and Jeanne Tripplehorn, *The Firm* was an immediate hit. It grossed $7.2 million on its opening day. The final script, however, altered the conclusion of Grisham's story. In the book, Mitch McDeere flees from both the mob and the FBI. In the movie, McDeere stands his ground to confront his enemies. This was supposedly a more agreeable conclusion for moviegoers. Despite the changes to his story, Grisham was pleased with the film overall.

While other Grisham projects were headed for the screen—director Joel Schumacher had started filming *The Client*—one property remained off limits: *A Time to Kill.* Agent Jay Garon had received eight offers from various producers for the rights to Grisham's first novel. But for now, Grisham was reluctant to sell. "[*A Time to Kill*] is very personal to me," he said. "I just want it done right." Grisham's favorite of all his books remained one of the most sought after stories in Hollywood.

His current manuscript, *The Chamber*, was also taking on great meaning to Grisham. The title refers to the gas chamber, and in this novel, the author addresses the difficult issue of capital punishment. It's the story of seventy-year-old Sam Cayhall, a Ku Klux Klansman who is on death row for the murder of two young sons of a Jewish attorney.

Just one month before the execution, a young Chicago lawyer named Adam Hall arrives. Hall tries to reverse the death sentence of the old man, who turns out to be his grandfather. Hall despises Sam, a hateful bigot who committed terrible acts. At the same time, Hall opposes the death penalty.

Grisham was similarly divided over the issue. On one hand he saw capital punishment as justice served. But he also felt it was wrong. To research his book, Grisham visited the Mississippi State Penitentiary at Parchman, where he got a first-hand experience of death row.

There, Grisham spent time among convicted killers and learned thc stories of their victims. He studied every detail of the death chamber. He even had guards strap him onto an execution table so he could feel what that was like. These experiences haunted Grisham for a long time. His feelings about capital punishment, however, remained unsettled.

In late 1993, Grisham received an invitation to the White House, where he joined a select party of forty guests for a special screening of *The Pelican Brief.* The author had the place of honor next to President Bill Clinton and his wife, Hillary, and they shared a bucket of popcorn.

A fellow Democrat, Grisham had campaigned actively for Clinton in his run for the presidency. At some point in their correspondence, Grisham learned that he and the president shared more than Arkansas roots. They were actually distant cousins—one of Clinton's grandfathers was a Grisham.

Grisham should have been riding high. However, he was beginning to regret selling the rights to *The Chamber.* While he was working on the manuscript, Grisham said he received some unwanted advice from studio people, who gave him their ideas about what should be in the book. This infuriated the author. The studio wanted him to produce another of his trade-mark thrillers. But Grisham struck out in a different direction, focusing instead on the death penalty issue and the moral struggles of the young attorney.

Unlike his previous works, Grisham took a full nine months to write this challenging book. Doubleday had great faith in *The Chamber* and produced a whopping 2.5 million copies. It was believed to be the largest fiction first printing in history.

In the dead of night in May 1994, booksellers across America arranged stacks upon stacks of the latest Grisham novel. At the stroke of 12:00, the stores opened their doors to fans already lined up for the book's midnight release. "He's really the only author we'd even attempt something like this with," said Glenne Hemmerle, chairman of Crown Books, whose stores continued to sell books throughout the night.[5]

For his risky departure from the popular suspense formula, Grisham won wide praise. *The Chamber* "allows the author to do some of his best writing since [*A Time to Kill*]," wrote critic Mark Harris. Mel Koler in *Contemporary Southern Writers* said that of Grisham's work, *The Chamber*, along with *A Time to Kill*, "may well be his superior literary achievements."[6]

Nevertheless, Grisham was experiencing a downside to his tremendous popularity. "The loss of privacy really ambushed us," he said. " . . . I didn't realize I was such a private person, until I lost my privacy."[7] Reporters, fans, and the just plain curious mobbed him. His once peaceful Oxford home was now a regular stop on tours to Graceland, Elvis's home in nearby Memphis.

One day John and Renee were relaxing on their porch, when they spotted someone on the road staring at them through a telephoto lens. Even more shocking was the time they discovered a couple getting married in their field. Daily hordes of strangers forced the couple to erect gates around their property. But eventually the Grishams had had enough.

By June 1994, they had retreated to a 180-acre farm near Charlottesville, Virginia. The farm became a refuge for the Grishams, where they could escape the public eye.

In fact, Grisham seldom ventured very far from home. Every day, he received numerous invitations to events around the country, most of which he politely declined. He was quite proud of the fact that he had never spent more than ten days away from the American South. And it seemed that he intended to maintain his record. He especially shunned Hollywood, despite the success of films made of his books.

The third Grisham film, *The Client*, was released that July. Starring Susan Sarandon as Reggie Love, the movie was a critical success. Director Joel Schumacher's faithful adaptation became Grisham's favorite film version of his books. It also inspired the author to change his mind about selling the film rights to his first novel.

In August 1994—ten years after Grisham had begun his first book—Jay Garon accepted a $6 million offer from New Regency to film *A Time to Kill*. Schumacher was to direct. With his successful record in Hollywood, Grisham was now able to name his terms. He retained tight control over the script and even had a say over casting. He also required that the studio make a donation to his favorite charity, St. Jude's Hospital.

Grisham's career then took another turn. In August he became publisher of the Southern literary magazine called the *Oxford American*. The two-year-old quarterly was struggling financially, when Grisham came to its rescue and provided financial backing. But his involvement went beyond that of investor.

Together with *Oxford*'s editor and founder Marc Smirnoff, Grisham helped supervise editorial content of the magazine. Grisham had hit it off with Smirnoff when they first met in 1992, when the young bookstore clerk was just launching the *Oxford American*. Grisham had agreed to help out by contributing an article to the first issue.

"The idea of becoming associated with a young Southern magazine that is intent on exploring the region with excellent writers is just something I found irresistible," stated the enthusiastic new publisher.

In January 1995, Grisham was drawn back into the law. But this time he was being sued. Polly Nelson, who wrote a book about mass murderer Ted Bundy, claimed that Grisham illegally borrowed from her book in writing *The Chamber*. In a lawsuit filed in federal court, Nelson listed similarities between *The Chamber* and her book, *Defending the Devil*, based on her experience as Bundy's lawyer. An infamous killer, Bundy had been executed in Florida in 1989, after confessing to the grisly murders of twenty-three women.

Grisham's attorney, Bruce Sanford, dismissed the

The Rainmaker *was the top-selling hardcover of 1995, with 23 million copies sold.*

lawsuit, saying that his client had never heard of Nelson or her book. Moreover, *The Chamber* had been released two months before *Defending the Devil.*

A federal judge denied any similarities between the two books and decided in Grisham's favor. [Nelson pursued her case all the way to the Supreme Court, which decided in Grisham's favor in March 1998].

Like clockwork, 1995 saw the publication of another Grisham novel in the spring. In *The Rainmaker*, Rudy Baylor, a young lawyer, sues a major insurance company on behalf of a girl who is dying of leukemia. *The Rainmaker* may have lacked some of the pace of his earlier work. But critics noted Grisham's attempt to add something that had never before appeared in his books—humor.

The fans snatched up more than 2.3 million copies of *The Rainmaker*. It became the number-one best-selling hardcover of 1995, while another Grisham title, *The Chamber*, held the top spot on the paper-back list. With more than 55 million copies of his books in print, the publishing world declared Grisham "king" of the best-sellers.[8]

9

Turning Pages

In August 1995, literary agent Jay Garon died suddenly of a heart attack. He was seventy-one. Garon had discovered John Grisham in 1984 and managed his career ever since. The publishing world pondered the superstar author's next move.

Late in 1995, just as a television series based on *The Client* was set to air, Grisham's longtime editor David Gernert made a big announcement. He was stepping down as editor in chief of Doubleday in November to open a new literary agency. His first client was John Grisham.

The new arrangement was a logical one. David Gernert had helped shape every Grisham manuscript since *The Firm*. Besides Renee, Gernert was the author's most trusted advisor. Grisham had faithfully followed his editor's advice with every novel, and it had paid off.

In fact, a Grisham story must meet with the approval of Renee, then Gernert, before he even starts writing a book. Grisham admits that he has junked several ideas, based on discussions with Gernert. As for Renee, she expresses her disapproval simply by flinging the offending work across the room.

So when he sits down to write, Grisham says, "I'm pretty secure . . . because the story has already been tested, talked about and kicked around."[1] Then Grisham spends a great deal of care in developing an outline that emphasizes a fast-moving plot. "Turning pages . . . You must have a story that makes the reader turn the pages," he said.[2]

Despite his success—*Forbes* magazine estimated his 1996 income at $43 million—Grisham continued to drive himself. He maintained the same strict writing schedule he had established with his first book, starting work at 5:00 A.M. Grisham cannot stand lazy writers who do not share his self-discipline. If he did not produce four or five pages by 7:30 in the morning, he did not consider it a good day. In early 1996, however, Grisham's writing schedule was interrupted by two legal incidents that commanded his attention.

In January, John Grisham returned to try a court case for the first time in five years. Although it meant delaying his next book, he would keep a commitment he had made to take the case in 1991, just after *The Firm* was published. Representing the widow of train brakeman John Wayne King, Grisham would pursue a wrongful death lawsuit against the railway.

The small courtroom was packed with spectators and the press, eager to watch the best-selling author in action. Using a model of a railroad yard, Grisham demonstrated how King was tragically crushed between two cars. Illinois Central Railroad was responsible, he argued, due to malfunctioning equipment and mistakes made by the railway's workers. King's death "could easily have been stopped," Grisham stated to the jury. "And it should have been stopped."[3]

After two hours of deliberation, the jury awarded King's widow more than $680,000. A relieved Grisham responded by saying, "I'm tickled to death. It's the biggest verdict I've ever gotten."[4]

In February 1996, Grisham filed a lawsuit of his own against his late agent, Jay Garon. Grisham charged that Garon and Elliot Lefkowitz, his former attorney, had accepted secret payments from movie producers during negotiations involving Grisham's work. Grisham sought an unspecified amount in damages, as well as an end to his contract with the Jay Garon–Brooke agency, which had continued to collect commissions on Grisham books Garon had negotiated before his death. Up until the lawsuit, it appeared as if Grisham and Garon had had a good relationship. "I regret matters have reached this point," was all Grisham would say, as Garon's agency settled for an undisclosed amount.[5]

Fame and money—and all that comes with it—had forced Grisham and his wife to "circle the wagons."

Together they worked to preserve their family's interests and keep the children's lives as normal as possible. They had never been closer, said Grisham.[6]

Despite his family's support, Grisham sometimes struggled with his success. "I go for long walks in the woods a lot, and I ask myself if I'm handling it the way it ought to be handled," he said. "I don't know why it happened to me. God has a purpose for it. We are able to contribute an awful lot of money to his work, and maybe that's why."[7]

Grisham and Renee believed strongly in their obligation to use their wealth to help others. They made regular donations through the church. They also supported a variety of other causes, from the restoration of Faulkner's home, Rowan Oak, to the funding of special programs at the University of Mississippi. In April 1996, Grisham made a unique gift to his Virginia community that became a labor of love.

When Grisham realized their farm was twenty miles from the nearest ball field, the devoted baseball fan sprang into action. He bought enough land to construct a couple of practice fields for local teams. But that was only the beginning. Grisham's project soon evolved into Cove Creek Park, a six-field complex that would serve hundreds of children from across the region.

Grisham devoted himself to his beloved park, per-forming all sorts of duties, from commissioner to groundskeeper. He was often seen out by himself, mowing the grass, laying chalk lines, or just gazing out onto the manicured field.

John Grisham contributed funds to help restore Rowan Oak, William Faulkner's home in Oxford, Mississippi.

Grisham was all business when discussing his career. But his tone softened whenever the conversation turned to baseball. "This is my game," Grisham told a reporter, smiling. "My childhood was spent in ballparks . . . We were either playing or watching. This is just my game."[8]

Grisham was pleased that his kids had inherited his passion for baseball. He had coached both Ty and Shea's teams for years, arranging his writing schedule around the Little League season. Grisham's record, however, threatened his coaching career. "I built a ballpark and I'm 0-3," admitted Grisham. "The

John Grisham offers some advice to his son Ty at a Little League baseball game between Grisham's Cove Creek White Sox and the Oxford Allstars in 1997.

good thing about baseball, is that there's always another day," he added, hopefully.[9]

The Runaway Jury—Grisham's seventh novel— was released in May 1996. Typically, the story centers on a court case, this time involving the widow of a lung cancer victim who sues the big tobacco companies over her husband's death. "Big Tobacco" hires a cunning lawyer, Rankin Fitch, to try and influence the jury, adding a dark twist to the courtroom thriller. Critics praised Grisham's treatment of an important issue.

Grisham's next legal drama began on the pages of the *Oxford American*. In a spring 1996 article, Grisham wrote about a violent 1995 spree in which two teenagers shot and killed his friend, Bill Savage, in Hernando, Mississippi. The young murderers, Sarah Edmonson and Ben Darras, then shot store clerk Patsy Byers, leaving her paralyzed.

Edmonson and Darras later confessed and said that before the shootings, they had taken LSD and watched the film *Natural Born Killers*. They had viewed the movie—about the murderous rampage of two teenagers—countless times. Grisham was outraged at the senseless murders. He had known Savage from years ago, when the cotton gin manager had encouraged John to enter politics.

Grisham believed the film's director, Oliver Stone, should be legally accountable for the violence inspired by his work. *Natural Born Killers* is "a movie made with the intent of glorifying random murder," wrote Grisham. He blasted Stone as an artist who "can't be bothered with the effects of what he produces." If

Stone were to lose a million-dollar product-liability lawsuit, wrote Grisham, "the party will be over."[10]

Stone called the charges "ridiculously bizarre" in a reply published in *LA Weekly*. The director struck back at Grisham, questioning the morality of the novelist's own work. Legal experts believed that Stone was protected by the First Amendment, which guarantees freedom of speech. Nevertheless, an attorney for the victim, Patsy Byers, filed a lawsuit against Stone and Warner Brothers. The suit and its subsequent appeal both failed.

Grisham's feud with Stone contributed to the ongoing national controversy over violence in the media, and it did not end there. In July 1996, actor Woody Harrelson claimed that Grisham had rejected him for the lead in *A Time to Kill* because he had starred in *Natural Born Killers*. Grisham denied the accusation. The part of Jake Brigance went instead to then relatively unknown actor Matthew McConaughey.

In August 1996, Grisham set another record in Hollywood, when Warner Brothers bought film rights to *The Runaway Jury* for $8 million. It would be the third time that Joel Schumacher and Grisham worked together on a film.

The Grisham movie machine went into high gear in October 1996. The long-awaited movie version of *A Time to Kill* was scheduled to hit theaters. That same month, *The Rainmaker* began filming in Memphis under the direction of Francis Ford Coppola, the legendary creator of The Godfather films. *A Time to Kill* featured Samuel L. Jackson, Sandra Bullock, and

McConaughey. The movie would rake in $110 million and earn Grisham his first feature credit as producer.

The author was not as pleased with director James Foley's interpretation of *The Chamber*, featuring Gene Hackman and Chris O'Donnell, which also opened in October. "I am happy to say that I had nothing to do with the making of *The Chamber*," stated Grisham. "I think it's best if I leave it at that."

Despite his disappointment, Grisham remained philosophical about the movies. He had taken to heart some advice Stephen King gave him years ago. "He said when you deal with Hollywood, get all the money you can up front and then kiss your book

John Grisham (fourth from left) appeared with winners of the 1998 Master Teacher Awards at Mississippi State University.

goodbye," recalled Grisham. "It's just a movie, OK? It's not the book. And if you don't like that, then don't do it. Nobody forces you to sell your book to Hollywood."[11]

But, the popularity of the Grisham movies, otherwise known as "Grishamizations," caused the author some concern. He felt that *A Time to Kill* and *The Chamber* were released too close together. Moreover, the stories were very similar—both were based in Mississippi and dealt with the Ku Klux Klan. He also feared that people would get the impression that the state was filled with Klansmen.

Indeed, with so many of his works in circulation, Grisham may have suffered from overexposure. Nevertheless, the hard-working writer proceeded on schedule with another book.

Beginning at 12:01 A.M. on February 12, 1997, eager fans went online to preview the first chapter of Grisham's new novel, *The Partner*. The Grisham page on the America Online Web site received 80,000 visits on the first day alone. As one observer put it, that was enough people to fill Yankee Stadium and Fenway Park.[12] The hardbound edition of *The Partner* shipped to bookstores in March, and soon climbed to the number-one spot on *The New York Times* bestseller list.

Inspired by an actual event, *The Partner* involves a lawyer, Patrick Lanigan, who fakes his own death in order to make off with $90 million. Lanigan flees Mississippi for Brazil, a setting Grisham based on his own missionary experiences.

Grisham recalled a tale he had heard in the village

of Ponta Pora, near Paraguay. A Baptist missionary there told him about a local café, in a town where some elderly men would meet for lunch. The men spoke in German—they were old Nazis. Grisham imagined how anyone on the run would find South America an ideal place to hide. And so was born the idea for *The Partner.*

Readers of this book found themselves rooting for a rather shady character in Lanigan. This makes for a more interesting story, according to Grisham. The author likes his heroes flawed "because we're all flawed; none of us are above temptation," he explained. "I get them in even more trouble, make them make choices, watch them screw up or work themselves free, and in so doing take readers for a ride."[13]

Reviewer Robert Drake called *The Partner* "a fine book, wholly satisfying, and a superb example of a masterful storyteller's prowess captured at its peak."[14]

A Street Lawyer, A Farm Boy, and A Thriller

Grisham left the high-priced lawyers and million-dollar schemes behind to explore a completely different world in his next book. As someone who had grown up in the rural South, Grisham had not been very aware of the homeless. But his career as a writer had brought him to the streets of New York, Chicago, and other big cities, where he encountered the issue firsthand.

Grisham was walking in New York one day, when suddenly an angry man confronted him, asking for money. The man followed Grisham, who quickened his pace to get away. At that point, Grisham did not give any more thought to the real problem of home-lessness. He was simply more fearful of panhandlers.

But Grisham's experience did fire his writer's

imagination. He began a story about a high-powered, young attorney who survives a violent encounter with a street person and becomes an advocate for the poor. Grisham soon realized he knew little about the subject.

In the spring of 1997, Grisham went to research the world of the homeless, just a two-hour drive from his Virginia home. In Washington, D.C., he met real public advocate lawyers, who took him to shelters, soup kitchens, and parks where people lived. What he saw left Grisham stunned.

"I met women whose children had been taken away because they couldn't feed and clothe them," he said. "I almost froze on a park bench one night as I tried to strike up a conversation with a homeless man who suspected I was from the IRS."[1] At one shelter, Grisham saw a frightened young mother arrive with three small children. The youngsters attacked a pile of peanut butter sandwiches, as if they had not eaten in days.

"It was a very sad thing to watch," said Grisham. "And I had to remind myself that I was sitting in the nation's capitol in the wealthiest country this world has ever known. It's a different level of society that most of us don't want to see or don't want to acknowledge."[2]

The first chapter of *The Street Lawyer* premiered online in late February 1998. The gripping opening is classic Grisham. An armed, homeless man enters a prominent Washington, D.C., law firm and seizes nine hostages. A sniper's bullet ends the siege violently, leaving attorney Michael Brock among the survivors.

The shaken Brock is compelled to learn more about his mysterious attacker and how he ended up on the street. During the course of his investigation, Brock begins to question his own values and ends up quitting his high-power job to devote his skills to helping defend the poor.

Brock's discovery of an illegal eviction involving his own law firm delivers all the excitement that readers had come to expect from a Grisham thriller. But *The Street Lawyer* is also filled with vivid details and insight that reveal the plight of the homeless.

Although Grisham's handling of Brock's personal transformation was slammed by critics as rather unconvincing, others liked Grisham's sensitive and knowledgeable handling of the issue. Topics important to Grisham had become a traditional element in many of his works, from capital punishment in *The Chamber* and insurance fraud in *The Rainmaker*, to Big Tobacco in *The Runaway Jury*. In fact, Grisham once said that he probably would not be a novelist if it were not for a concern for social justice.[3]

True to form, Grisham incorporated another big topic in his next novel, *The Testament*, which was released in spring 1999. This time he wove into his story the preservation of the Brazilian wetlands. Grisham is careful, however, not to preach too much in his books. It is the story, above else, that drives his work. But Grisham's next tale was like nothing he had ever attempted before.

In the summer of 1999, a package arrived at the desk of Marc Smirnoff, editor of the *Oxford American*. Smirnoff opened it to find a manuscript with an

Grisham appeared at a ribbon-cutting ceremony for the John Grisham Room at Mississippi State University.

attached note that said "Please read this and let me know what you think."[4] It was the first hundred pages of a new novel by John Grisham.

A Painted House is the fictional memoir of a seven-year-old farm boy growing up in rural Arkansas in the 1950s. Without a lawyer in sight, the story was a dramatic new turn for the best-selling author. In another twist, Grisham asked Smirnoff if he would consider publishing the novel, chapter by chapter, in the magazine. Serializations, once popular in the nineteenth century, had not been done in some time.

The first of six installments of *A Painted House*

appeared in the January/February 2000 issue of the *Oxford American*. It was a great boost for the tiny magazine, which upped its print run from 50,000 to a quarter of a million copies for this issue. Grisham wrote each installment in time for publication in the magazine, which would publish the entire novel over the course of the year.

Meanwhile, Grisham's eleventh book came out that February. *The Brethren* involves three imprisoned judges who launch a black-mailing scam. The Brethren, as they call themselves, trap victims who respond to ads placed in a gay magazine. Their scam eventually snags a presidential candidate in a plot *Entertainment Weekly* called "wacky." Nevertheless, *The Brethren* topped the charts of online retailer Amazon.com two weeks before it went on sale in bookstores.

By producing a bestseller every year, Grisham had gained a momentum that launched him into publishing's record books. *Publishers Weekly* officially declared him the best-selling author of the 1990s. His total sales for the decade: 60,742,288 copies.[5] Horror writer Stephen King took second place with 38.3 million copies. King's sales, while impressive, paled in comparison to Grisham's.

So it was even more surprising that Grisham would turn away from legal thrillers and attempt such a different novel in *A Painted House*. Observers noted the risk Grisham was taking and were impressed. "Most authors don't do this," said Nancy Rutland, a New Mexico bookseller. Doubleday showed their confidence in *A Painted House* by ordering a first printing of 2.8 million copies, just as they had done with Grisham's last five books.

Grisham's novel was inspired by his own childhood in Black Oak, Arkansas, where he lived the first seven years of his life. Loosely based on family stories Grisham had heard as a child, *A Painted House* details life in a cotton farming community, as seen through the eyes of a baseball-obsessed young boy.

Just as the book was released in February 2001, John Grisham made a unique gift to the University of Mississippi, where he had earned his law degree. He and Renee sponsored the Civil Law Clinic, a program that gave law students practical experience, while providing the poor with free legal assistance.

With Grisham's funding, a professor was hired to help supervise students, who represented clients in actual cases. The clinic helped needy clients with child support and domestic violence cases, among other issues.

Meanwhile, *A Painted House* met with mixed reviews. Janet Maslin in *The New York Times* cited the book's slow pace, saying that talk about the weather takes up a lot of space in *A Painted House* "because there is so little else going on."[6] "I gave up on those folks a long time ago," was all Grisham had to say about the critics. Grisham made appearances to promote the book, then turned his attention to the local baseball season.

For years Grisham had dreamed of creating a baseball story. Those dreams were finally realized in May, when filming began on *Mickey*. The original Grisham screenplay tells the story of a father and son who want one more season of Little League. Grisham and film director Hugh Wilson, his friend and Virginia neighbor, financed the film themselves.

Grisham played a small part in the film as the Little League commissioner. He says that when he found out "that they were going to pay an actor $10,000 bucks to do something I do every year at the park, I said 'Hugh, I'm not going to waste $10,000 bucks. I can do this in my sleep.'"[7] Wilson said okay, and Grisham thoroughly enjoyed the experience. *Mickey* starred Harry Connick, Jr., and was originally slated to open in late 2002.

Grisham was preparing for the publication of his next book, when tragedy struck on September 11, 2001. Three airplanes hijacked by terrorists slammed into New York's World Trade Center and the Pentagon in Washington, D.C., killing more than three thousand people.

A stunned Grisham wanted somehow to contribute to the recovery. So he decided to donate the royalties from the sale of his next book, a lighthearted Christmas story, to a scholarship fund for children who lost their parents in the attacks.

In *Skipping Christmas*, released in November 2001, accountant Luther Krank is fed up with the materialism of the season. So he and his wife agree not to celebrate Christmas. Or at least they try. "Think of all the things you would have to do to skip Christmas, just to avoid it, it really can't be done, not in our culture and society," said Grisham. "And so it became a pretty funny story."[8]

Grisham said he had once tried to skip the holiday

Grisham put aside his legal-thriller style to write Skipping Christmas *in 2001. It soon joined many of his other books on the best-seller list.*

at his own house, but it did not go over too well with his family. *Skipping Christmas* became a best-seller. But fans began to wonder if John Grisham would ever produce another legal thriller.

In February 2002, Grisham responded with his fourteenth book, *The Summons.* The story's hero, Ray Atlee, returns to his family's home in Clanton, Mississippi, after receiving a letter from his gravely ill father, a respected judge. When Ray arrives, he discovers his father's body, along with twenty-seven boxes stuffed with $3.12 million in cash. What Ray does with the money and the shocking family secret that is revealed in the process is a classic Grisham thrill ride. *The Summons* marked John Grisham's return to the genre that made him famous.

In May, John Grisham returned to his alma mater, Mississippi State University. Grisham and Renee had given generously to MSU over the past decade, sponsoring student scholarships and a writer-in-residence program. This time they were donating $1.5 million to honor outstanding teachers. The first winners of $10,000 Grisham Teaching Excellence Awards were honored in the fall of 2002.

MSU's Mitchell Memorial Library also houses the John Grisham Room, a collection of manuscripts, personal papers, and memorabilia related to his incredible career. It draws visitors from around the world, as well as local schoolchildren, who go there to learn the remarkable story of the Mississippi author who became the best-selling novelist of all time.

John Grisham, Superstar Author

"John Grisham is a rock star," declared one observer.[1] Indeed, the country lawyer who once scribbled stories on legal pads in his spare time has achieved unprecedented fame. Walk down any beach or through any airport, and he is there, in paperback after paperback. "I know this is all temporary," Grisham once said of his astounding career. "I'm a famous writer in a country where few people read."[2]

But Grisham has single-handedly done his best to turn that around. People flood into bookstores the first day his novels go on sale, reported Barnes & Noble. One quarter of those who purchase a new Grisham hardcover also buy at least one other book at the same time.[3] Grisham leads millions of people to read.

What are the reasons for his success? Publishers wish they knew the secret. As for Grisham, he believes that Americans are simply fascinated with the law. "We hate lawyers, but we love stories about 'em," he said.[4] Readers also love a classic struggle of good against evil, conspiracies, and plots that move at breakneck speed.

Grisham gives readers what they want. He admits sacrificing story and character development to keep the plot moving and the audience turning pages. The absence of sex and violence also makes his books appropriate for more readers. Besides which, said Grisham, "I couldn't write a book that I would be embarrassed for my kids to read a few years from now. Plus my mother would kill me."[5]

Grisham also appeals to people on a personal level. One critic wrote: "You don't have to be an admirer of his prose or to have read too far into his novels to admire his humanity."[6] Fans note his commitment to his family and community. They also see him donating his time and money to good causes, from church missions and writing scholarships to local baseball and literacy programs.

Grisham's best friends have been his best friends since long before he was famous. Everyone says that fame has not changed him.

He is reserved by nature, but unfailingly polite. Those lucky enough to get into his book signings are always struck by how nice he is. He is the type of

Grisham spoke at Mississippi State University commencement in 1992. He is shown here with MSU president Don Zacharias.

person who still corresponds with his high school English teacher. Francis McGuffey comes to see him whenever he signs books in Memphis.

Grisham says that he writes for his readers, and book signings are an opportunity to return their admiration and respect. He speaks to each fan and carefully considers his or her comments. But not so the critics. Negative reviews still irk him.

All he is trying to do, says Grisham, is write good popular fiction. That has been his goal since *The Firm.* "Only now I want the book I'm writing now to be better than the book I wrote last year," he said. This self-taught writer continues to work at his craft. Grisham's goal remains to write as clearly as John Steinbeck. So every few years, he rereads *The Grapes of Wrath* for inspiration.

Grisham's hard work has won the respect of his colleagues. Novelist Larry Brown believes Grisham has earned his success. "He paid his dues," said Brown. "He works harder than I do."[7]

But along with success comes enormous pressure. Grisham has committed to producing a novel a year. Grisham's publisher, the booksellers, and others

John Grisham posed on the set of Mickey. *Grisham wrote the original screenplay about a father and son who want to play one more season of Little League together.*

in the "Grisham business" all have high expectations that each book will be another best-seller.

Grisham copes with the demands, for now. "When I reach a point to where I'm cranking out the books simply because of my name, I hope I have the sense to quit," he said.[8] Until then Grisham has plenty of ideas. He has several books that he is just anxious to write.

Looking back at his life, Grisham realizes how taking a chance made all the difference. "I never planned to write books. I thought I'd be a lawyer for the rest of my life," he says. So Grisham advises young people not to be too rigid in their future plans. "It's important to have goals and work hard for them," he says. "But life has a way of presenting opportunities . . . It will be up to you to take a chance, to be bold, to have faith, and go for it."[9] Like he once did.

Chronology

1955—Born on February 8, in Jonesboro, Arkansas.

1967—Moves to Southaven, Mississippi.

1973—Graduates from Southaven High School; enters Northwest Mississippi Junior College.

1974—Transfers to Delta State University.

1975—Enters Mississippi State University.

1977—Earns a B.S. degree in accounting.

1978—Enters the University of Mississippi Law School.

1981—Graduates from the University of Mississippi Law School; marries Renee Jones.

1983—Elected to Mississippi state legislature; birth of son, Ty.

1984—Begins writing first book.

1986—Birth of daughter, Shea.

1987—Completes manuscript for *A Time to Kill*; signs a contract with agent Jay Garon.

1988—Signs contract with Wynwood Press for his first book; reelected to second term.

1989—*A Time to Kill* is published.

1990—Sells film rights to *The Firm*; builds dream home in Oxford, Mississippi; quits law practice; resigns from legislature.

1991—*The Firm* is published; sells film rights to *The Pelican Brief* before the manuscript is finished.

1992—*The Pelican Brief* becomes the number one best-seller; sells film rights to *The Client* at a record $2.5 million.

1993—Embarks on mission to Brazil; attends premiere of *The Firm.*

1994—*The Chamber* is published; retreats to farm in Charlottesville, Virginia; becomes publisher of the *Oxford American.*

1995—Garon dies; editor David Gernert assumes role.

1996—Returns to try court case; builds youth baseball complex; *The Runaway Jury* is published; sues Garon agency; attacks director Oliver Stone in press over film violence.

1997—*The Partner* is published.

1998—*The Street Lawyer* is published.

1999—*The Brethren* is published; the *Oxford American* publishes *A Painted House* in serial form.

2000—Declared best-selling author of the 1990s.

2001—*A Painted House,* and *Skipping Christmas* are published.

2002—*The Summons* is published.

2003—*The King of Torts* is published.

Books by John Grisham

A Time to Kill, 1989

The Firm, 1991

The Pelican Brief, 1992

The Client, 1993

The Chamber, 1994

The Rainmaker, 1995

The Runaway Jury, 1996

The Partner, 1997

The Street Lawyer, 1998

The Testament, 1999

The Brethren, 2000

A Painted House, 2001

Skipping Christmas, 2001

The Summons, 2002

The King of Torts, 2003

Chapter Notes

Chapter 1. Southern Loyalty Tour

1. Michael Selden, "Celebrity Square," (Glasgow) *Evening Times*, Glasgow, Scotland, February 24, 2001, p. 8.

2. Lisa Marton, "A Sign from Grisham: Prolific author pays his dues," *The Arkansas Democrat-Gazette*, March 10, 1998, p. E1.

Chapter 2. Dreams of Glory

1. Sammy McDavid, "A Time To Write," *Mississippi State Alumnus*, Winter 1990, pp. 13–16.

2. Kim Hubbard, "Tales Out of Court," *People Weekly*, March 16, 1992, p. 43.

3. Charles Osgood, "A Time to Remember: Oxford, Miss. Magazine Publishes a John Grisham Serial About a Young Farm Boy," *CBS Sunday Morning*, February 13, 2000.

4. Will Norton, "Why John Grisham Teaches Sunday School," *Christianity Today*, October 3, 1994, pp. 14–15.

5. John Grisham, "Mothers," *The Saturday Evening Post*, May/June 1999, p. 48.

6. Robin Street, "The Grisham Brief," *Writer's Digest*, July 1993, p. 33.

7. John Grisham, "John Grisham Interview," n.d., <http://members.aol.com/fictwri/jg.html>, n.d. February 8, 2002.

8. Ibid.

9. McDavid, pp. 13–16.

Chapter 3. Grisham Gets Serious

1. John Grisham, "John Grisham describes his undergraduate days at Mississippi State University," *Mississippi State Alumnus*, Winter 1991, <http://nt.library.msstate.edu/grisham_home/Journey_end.html>, (April 26, 2001).

2. Patty Archer, "Grisham Traces His Success to University Economics Class: Debate Was the Key," *Sun Herald*, Biloxi, Miss., February 23, 1997, p. H3.

3. Grisham.

4. Mary Beth Pringle, *John Grisham: A Critical Companion*, (Westport, Conn.: Greenwood Publishing, 1997), p. 2.

5. Will Norton, "Why John Grisham Teaches Sunday School," *Christianity Today*, October 3, 1994, pp.14–15.

6. Sarah Booth Conroy, "The Tort Story Writer," *The Washington Post*, March 28, 1992, p. C1.

7. "The first 'client' most trying for young Grisham," *The Herald-Sun* Durham, N.C., March 24, 1996, p. E4.

8. Michelle Bearden, "PW Interviews John Grisham," *Publisher's Weekly*, February 23, 1993, p. 70.

9. Conroy.

Chapter 4. First-Time Author

1. Mel Koler, "John Grisham," *Contemporary Southern Writers*, (Detroit: St. James Press, 1999), p. 171.

2. Ibid.

3. Robin Street, "The Grisham Brief," *Writer's Digest*, July 1993, pp. 32–34.

4. Kim Hubbard, "Tales Out of Court," *People Weekly*, March 16, 1992, p. 43.

5. Michelle Bearden, "PW Interviews: John Grisham," *Publisher's Weekly*, February 23, 1993, p. 70.

6. John Grisham, *A Time to Kill*, (New York: Wynwood Press, 1989), pp. ix–xi.

7. Sammy McDavid, "A Time To Write," *Mississippi State Alumnus*, Winter 1990, pp. 13–16.

8. Daniel Wise, "'The Firm' Lets Lawyer-Author Quit Practice for Fiction-Writing," *New York Law Journal*, April 18, 1991, p. 1.

9. Ibid., p. 27.

10. Ibid., pp ix–xi.

11. Tom Mathews, "Book 'Em," *Newsweek*, March 15, 1993, pp. 79-81.

12. "John Grisham Recalls No-shows at 1st Signing," *Baton Rouge Advocate*, February 11, 1999, p. 3A.

13. David Keymer, "A Time to Kill," *Library Journal*, June 15, 1989, p. 80.

14. Judith Graham, ed., "John Grisham," *Current Biography Yearbook 1993* (New York: H. W. Wilson Company, 1993), p. 222.

Chapter 5. The Big Break

1. Michelle Bearden, "PW Interviews: John Grisham," *Publisher's Weekly*, February 22, 1993, p. 70.

2. Tom Mathews, "Book 'Em," *Newsweek*, March 15, 1993, pp. 79–81.

3. Ibid., pp. 79–81.

4. Robin Street, "The Grisham Brief," *Writer's Digest*, July 1993, pp. 32–34.

5. Mathews, pp. 79–81.

6. Kelli Pryor, "'The Firm' and the Farm," *Entertainment Weekly*, August 2, 1991, <http://www.ew.com/ew/report/0,6115,315012~7|6574||0~00.html>, (April 29, 2002).

7. Hubbard, Kim "Tales Out of Court," *People Weekly*, March 16, 1992, p. 43.

8. *Current Biography Yearbook*, (New York: H. W. Wilson Company, 1993), p. 222.

9. "Southaven Lawmaker Steps Down, Citing Time Constraints," *The Commercial Appeal*, Memphis, Tenn., September 6, 1990, p. A17.

10. Sammy McDavid, "A Time To Write," *Mississippi State Alumnus*, Winter 1990, pp. 13–16.

Chapter 6. Like a Whirlwind

1. Pagan Kennedy, "A review of *The Firm,*" *VLS,* July–August 1991, p. 7.

2. Peter S. Prescott, "Murky Maneuvers in a Lethal Law Firm," *Newsweek,* February 25, 1991, p. 63.

3. Bill Brashler, "Corporate Lawyers Who Lead Wild Lives," *Chicago Tribune,* February 24, 1991, p. 6.

4. "John Grisham Interview," <http://members.aol.com/fictwri/jg/html>, (April 29, 2002).

5. Erika Holzer, "Erika Holzer Interviews John Grisham," *New York Law Journal,* March 9, 1992, p. 2.

6. Michelle Bearden, "PW Interviews John Grisham," *Publisher's Weekly,* February 23, 1993, p. 70.

7. Don O'Briant, "Author of Best-selling Thriller is Just a Mississippi Family Man," *Atlanta Constitution,* April 16, 1991, p. C1.

8. Kim Hubbard, "Tales Out of Court," *People Weekly,* March 16, 1992, p. 43.

9. O'Briant, p. C1.

10. Fredric Koeppel, "Mississippi's Real Thriller is Rapid Rise of Bestseller," *The Commercial Appeal,* Memphis, Tenn., March 20, 1991, p. A 1.

11. Daisy Maryles, "Behind the Bestsellers," *Publishers Weekly,* February 16, 1998, p. 111.

12. John Grisham Interview. <http://members.aol.com/fictwri/jg.html>, (April 29, 2002).

Chapter 7. John Grisham Knocks Out John Grisham

1. Daniel Jones and John D. Jorgenson, eds., "John Grisham," *Contemporary Authors* (Detroit: Gale Research), 1999, p. 227.

2. Ann Oldenburg, "A Time for Grisham," *USA Today,* June 2, 1994, p. D1.

3. Mel Gussow, "Ex-Lawyer Gladly Takes the Money and Runs," *Richmond Times-Dispatch,* April 6, 1997, p. G1.

4. Erika Holzer, "Erika Holzer Interviews John Grisham," *New York Law Journal,* March 9, 1992. p. 2.

5. Elizabeth Sanger, "How the No. 2 Book Begat No. 1," *Newsday,* July 13, 1992, p. 33.

6. Mary George Beggs, "Book by Grisham Gains New Heights," *The Commercial Appeal,* Memphis, Tenn., July 22, 1992, p. C1.

7. Fredric Koeppel, "Bestseller!: Grisham Takes Modest Pleasure in Success," *The Commercial Appeal,* Memphis, Tenn., May 26, 1991, p. G1.

8. Susan Toepfer, "Talking With . . . John Grisham," *People Weekly,* March 15, 1993, pp. 27–28.

9. Robert W. Welkos, "'The Client' That's Worth $2.5 Million," *Los Angeles Times,* October 14, 1992, p. 1

10. Susan Toepfer, "Talking With . . . John Grisham," *People Weekly,* March 15, 1993, pp. 27–28.

11. Fredric Koeppel, "Grisham Sells Rights for 3rd Film," *The Commercial Appeal,* Memphis, Tenn., October 21, 1992, p. C1.

Chapter 8. The Grisham Business

1. Elizabeth Bernstein, "He Creates New Readers," *Publishers Weekly,* January 19, 1998, p. 251.

2. Lynn Smith, "Kids on Film: Does 'The Client' Go By the Book? Opposing Sides," *Los Angeles Times,* July 28, 1994, p. 16.

3. Marc Smirnoff, "Interview with John Grisham," *The Oxford American,* Issue #3, 1993, <http://www.oxfordamerican.com>.

4. Saundra Torry, "For Lawyers, Writing Can Be a Novel Experience—and Escape," *The Washington Post,* February 17, 1992, p. F5

5. Jonathan Freedland, "The Law Lord: Writing is Big Business for John Grisham," *The Guardian,* May 30, 1994, p. 2.

6. Mel Koler, *Contemporary Southern Writers* (Detroit: St. James Press, 1999), p. 171.

7. Donald V. Adderton, "Novelist Heads South in Wake of New Book," *Sun Herald,* Biloxi, Miss., May 31, 1996, p. C1.

8. Jocelyn McClurg, "A Repeat for Grisham with Two at No. 1 on 1995 Sales List," *The Hartford Courant,* March 24, 1996, p. G3.

Chapter 9. Turning Pages

1. Robin Street, "The Grisham Brief," *Writer's Digest,* July 1993, pp. 32–34.

2. Michael Selden, "'It's Not a Very Stressful Life' Novelist John Grisham earns pounds 28M a year, lives on 1,000 acres in Virginia with horses and his own baseball park, and works for three hours a day," *The Daily Telegraph,* February 13, 2001, p. 22.

3. Associated Press, "Jittery Grisham Puts Down Pen to Take Up Advocacy for Widow," *The Commercial Appeal,* Memphis, Tenn., January 23, 1996, B2

4. Jennifer Ferranti, "Grisham's Law," *The Saturday Evening Post,* March 13, 1997, p. 42.

5. "Grisham sues late agent, lawyer raked off profits, *The Commercial Appeal,* Memphis, Tenn., March 3, 1996, p. 1B

6. Ann Oldenburg, "A Time for Grisham," *USA Today,* June 2, 1994, p. 01D.

7. John Grisham, "Mothers," *The Saturday Evening Post,* vol. 271, no. 3, May/June 1999, pp. 48–49.

8. Bryan Mullen, "Author Grisham Loves his Baseball," *The Florida Times-Union,* March 13, 1998, p. C1.

9. Jerry Ratcliffe, "Author scores hit with ballpark," *Richmond Times-Dispatch,* April 28, 1996, p. C-2.

10. Elizabeth Gleick, "A Time to Sue," *Time,* June 17, 1996, p. 90.

11. Alan Strachan, "With One Book Turning Into a Series, Grisham Focuses on Next Novels," *The Vancouver Sun,* July 30, 1995, p. C9.

12. John Marshall, "Grisham Fans Already Have Sunk Teeth Into "The Partner" On Line, *Milwaukee Journal Sentinel*, February 22, 1997, p. 8.

13. "Amazon.com Interviews John Grisham," <http://www.amazon.co.uk/exec/obidos/tg/feature/-/137103/ref_ed_cp_I_2_21026-5520429-9510066> (January 6, 2003).

14. Daniel Jones and John D. Jorgenson, eds., "John Grisham," *Contemporary Authors, New Revision Series*, Vol., 69, (Detroit: Gale Research), 1999, p. 29.

Chapter 10. A Street Lawyer, A Farm Boy, and A Thriller

1. Grisham John. "Somewhere for Everyone," *Newsweek*, February 9, 1998, p. 14.

2. Ibid.

3. Mark Wingfield, "Author John Grisham sticks to his guns on sex and profanity," *The Arkansas Democrat-Gazette*, March 11, 2000, p. H5.

4. Charles Osgood, "A Time to Remember: Oxford, Miss. Magazine Publishes a John Grisham Serial About a Young Farm Boy," *CBS Sunday Morning*, February 13, 2000.

5. CNN, "Grisham ranks as top-selling author of decade," CNN.com Book News, December 31, 1999, <http://www.cnn.com/1999/books/news/12/31/1990.sellers/> (June 13, 2002).

6. Janet Maslin, "Books of the Times: Watching Grass Grow and Men Fight," *The New York Times*, February 8, 2001, p. E9.

7. Katie Couric, "John Grisham talks about his latest book, 'Skipping Christmas'," *NBC Today Show*, November 29, 2001.

8. Ibid.

Chapter 11. John Grisham, Superstar Author

1. Jonathan Freedland, "The Law Lord: Writing is Big Business for John Grisham," *The Guardian*, May 30, 1994, p. 2.

2. T. R. Pearson, "The Runaway Writer," *Harper's Bazaar*, March 1996, pp. 326–327.

3. Elizabeth Bernstein, "He Creates New Readers," *Publishers Weekly*, January 19, 1998, p. 251.

4. Jonathan Freedland, "The Law Lord: Writing is Big Business for John Grisham," *The Guardian*, May 30, 1994, p. 2.

5. Jennifer Ferranti, "Grisham's Law," *The Saturday Evening Post*, March 13, 1997, p. 42.

6. Dick Victory, "Conspiracies of Gold," *Washingtonian*, June 1998, pp. 37–41.

7. T.R. Pearson, "The Runaway Writer," *Harper's Bazaar*, March 1996, pp. 326–327.

8. Tom Mathews, "Book 'Em," *Newsweek*, March 15, 1993, p. 81.

9. John Grisham, "Mississippi State University Summer Commencement 1992—John Grisham's Remarks to Graduates," August 10, 1998, <http://library.msstate.edu/grisham_home/Best_plans.html>.

Further Reading

Books

Grisham, John. *A Painted House.* New York: Random House, 1999.

Pringle, Mary Beth. *John Grisham: A Critical Companion.* West Port, Conn.: Greenwood Publishing Group, 1997.

Waggett, Gerard J. *The John Grisham Companion: A Fan's Guide to His Novels, Films, Life, and Career.* Sacramento, Calif.: Citadel Press, 2002.

Internet Addresses

Bookreporter biography
<http://www.bookreporter.com/authors/au-grisham-john.asp>

John Grisham's Official Website
<http://www.randomhouse.com/features/grisham/books/summons/realread.html>

Mississippi State University on John Grisham
<http://nt.library.msstate.edu/grisham_home>

Index